MINDFULNESS

This books belongs to

Mindfulness is the key to harmony with life, requiring no excessive effort. It's the ability to focus on the present moment without judgment, as if everything depended on it. What matters is not what we pay attention to, but the process of attention itself.

The mind restlessly dreams and thinks, never stopping. We spend a lot of time worrying about the future and dwelling on the past. However, the present moment, the only time when we truly live, is often missed. Returning to mindfulness means returning to life, to its wonders and challenges.

We are taught to think, but not to be mindful. Therefore, we often suffer from endless thoughts that hinder sleep and lead to anxiety or depression. Mindfulness frees us from this narrow perspective of thinking and allows us to fully experience our lives.

Believe and act

Never give up

Dream and achieve

Be strong inside

Go after your dream

Be better every day

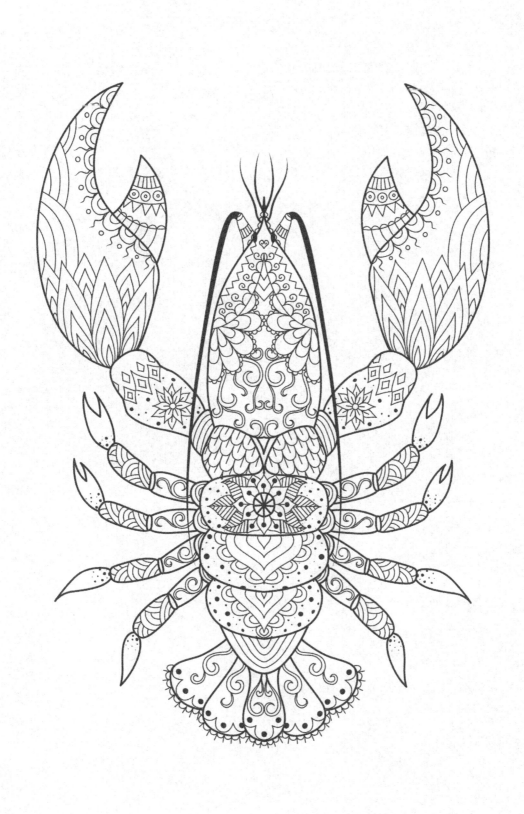

Make your choice boldly

Live a full life

Strive for the goal

Inspire and move forward

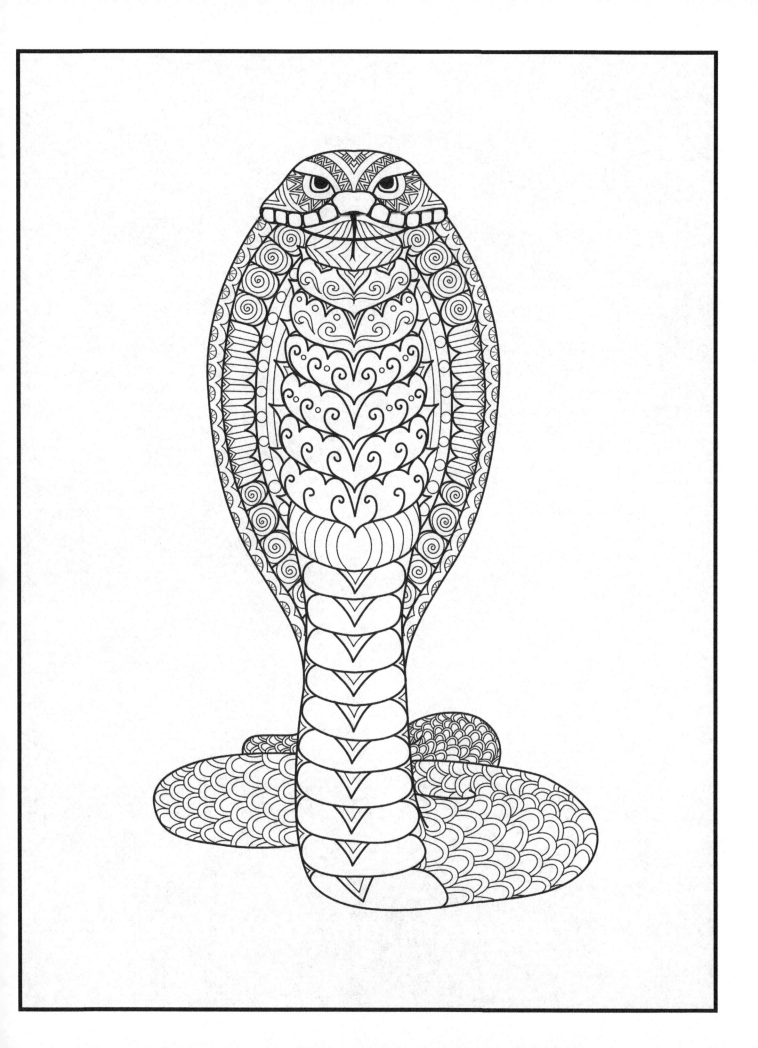

Believe in your strength

Stop waiting, start doing

Constantly develop

Break down walls of doubt

You can do anything

Be persistent and patient

Inspire others with actions

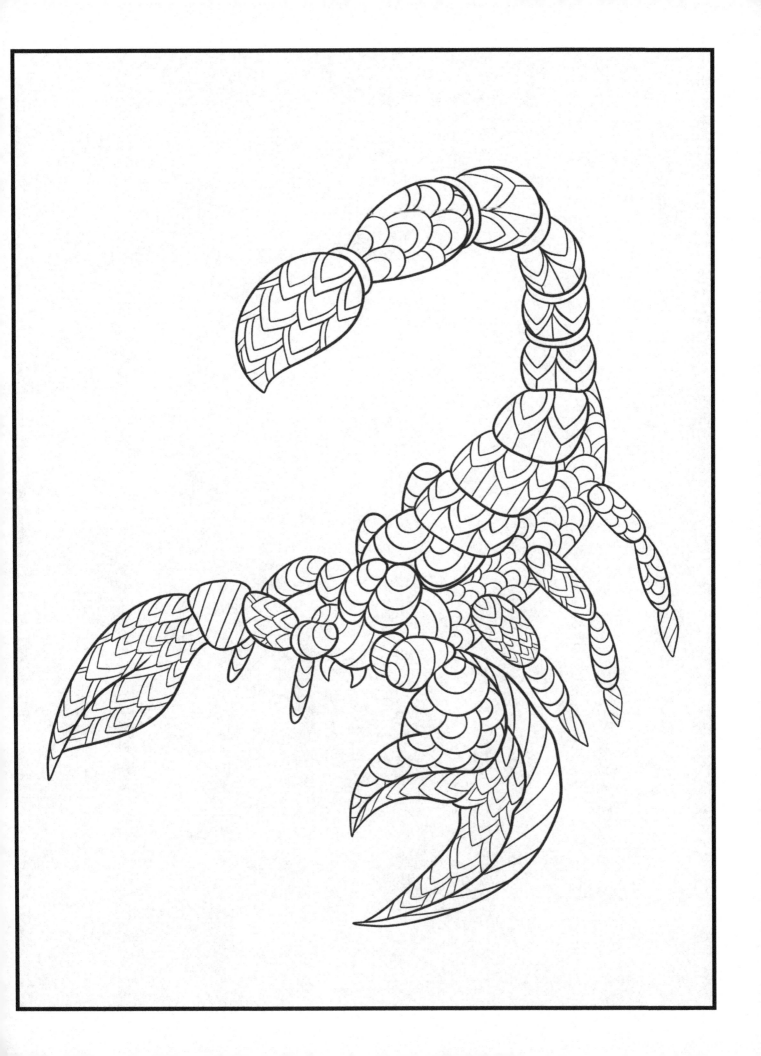

Love what you do

Conquer your fears

Strength is in your decisions

Believe in your dreams

Be bolder in actions

Don't look back

Overcome obstacles

Act with confidence

May your dreams come true

Find your inner fire

Be an inspiration to others

Follow your heart

Develop your potential

Be persistent in efforts

Take the first step boldly

Believe in your abilities

Be authentic in everything

Take small steps forward

Move forward with confidence

Show courage in actions

Keep the focus on the goal

Be stronger than your doubts

Unleash your potential

Set goals and act

Strive for new heights

Give it all you've got

Believe in your uniqueness

Don't be afraid to make mistakes

Be ready for changes

Overcome yourself every day

Never stop

Be proud of who you're becoming

Be inspired and inspire others

I am enough, just as I am

I am a warrior of light

I am a masterpiece in progress

Made in United States
Orlando, FL
22 July 2024

49395340R00063